ADVANCE PRAISE
FOR ABSOLUTION

I enjoyed, loved, was deeply touched, enthused, surprised … Suffice it to say, simply, BRAVO! This is a wonderful collection, well nuanced and of particular and special delight. I have read poetry but none from a newcomer who has managed to speak with so unwavering an ear to generous nuance. I must say that I was not expecting anything so startlingly distinctive. Love-and-relationship is often the subject of poetry, but Bonazzoli's voice is distinctive, profound and mature. I end with a holler-of-delight and a wish for continued sustenance that her work has offered me. Yummy!

—VENERABLE JANGCHUP PHELGYAL, Ph.D.
WRITER AND TIBETAN BUDDHIST MONK,
Vajrapani Monastery

The depth of Bonazzoli's spirituality is so evident, deep, beautiful and real. The passion deeply imbedded in these poems is captivating … and the strong emotions concerning life, death, sorrow, love, sex and the created world are breathtakingly evident.

—FATHER JIM CLIFFORD, OSA
Retired Director of Mission & Spiritual
Care, Providence Medford Medical Center

I love Dr. Bonazzoli's poetry. It moved me so much it left me speechless. In fact, these poems go beyond deeply moving. Here's how I recently described her work to colleagues: I only wish my own voice was so eloquent and rich. Her work brings me to the brink of melancholy but always on this side of hope—though sometimes I find it difficult to feel her soul so deeply. I found it impossible to read more than a few at a time without taking time out to both savor their wisdom and richness, as well as to personally reflect.

—LINDA PINKHAM,
editor, Linda Pinkham Publishing Services

Immediate and intimate, this winter-soul immersed me in the raw emotions of grief, loss and death. As I settled into her words, they then began to warm, budding with new expressions of life. A spring-soul emerged, filled with hope; exploring the sensual and relational contours of love. Her work is an engaging and elegant encounter with many of life's mysteries. Her honesty is refreshing.

—REV. DR. RANDOLPH T. MILLER,
Southern Oregon

Bonazzoli is a true Spiritual Warrior. In the more than 27 years I have known her I have witnessed first hand how she humbly walks the talk about self-awareness, acceptance, compassion and personal development. She has faced every personal challenge with courage and insight and has helped me find meaning and strength within my own life challenges as well. Her deep wells of wisdom are evident to all who are blessed to know her.

I recommend Absolution to all who want to learn from someone who truly lives a compassionate, aware and fully connected life. Savor her deeply personal poetry, and come to know her—perhaps in a different way than I have, but as a deep and profound blessing nonetheless.

—LLOYD NIRENBERG, Ph.D.,
Chief Investment Officer,
Rocket Science Capital Analytics

What a tour de force! What a courageous gift of courage Bonazzoli has so honestly and unabashedly given her readers by so nakedly sharing her love and her suffering! Her intimacy with Nature, the Divine, Lovers—all laid out in such a fully human way! At times I was not certain who was the lover....a person, Nature or the Divine....and that was not only perfect, it was also the beauty!

I could feel Bonazzoli's love and appreciation of every-thing....every experience.... from bliss to suffering and back to bliss....sense her profound awareness that we are the Love, we are the Oneness...and then feel her moving back to aware-ness of duality and suffering...back and forth and back again. And, I could feel her intimate openness with where she is at, and sense it in every word....

I loved it! Simply stunning!

TED T. SUNDINE, M.D., Ph.D.
Psychiatry and Neurology, Ashland, Oregon

There is a long and necessary genealogy of sensual spirituality … from the Song of Songs, to Hafiz, John of the Cross, Teresa of Avila, Rumi, and all those other lovers and prophets who have been ignited by Divine Love to communicate to the rest of us, who are living in the make-ends-meet world, what life can really be like. Absolution belongs to this illustrious list.

However, do not be misled. Bonazzoli's images are not photoshopped pictures of opulent window dressings. Grounded in the muck of suffering, uncertainty, and failure these poetic lines give birth to a lotus of searing rapture caressed by an unflinching honesty.

Do yourself a favor. Explore these windows into a true seeker's soul and discover your own. Your journey will not feel so lonely.

—Rev. Dr. Fred Grewe,
Hospice Chaplain and Author of
What the Dying Have Taught Me About Living

The first time I read these poems, which ride on the edge of death, life, and love, I did so straight through in one sitting, feeling myself being slowly and warmly enveloped in their passion, subtlety, raw power, and enigmatic mystery. Although Bonazzoli minces no words she never tells the full story—that story so deeply and sacredly known and lived by every mystic is far too ineffable for words. Yet she pierces the darkness that can't be broken, illuminates what cannot be lit. The extraordinary is rendered familiar and the familiar extraordinary. Simply beautiful, these poems live on the cutting edge of bearability. They are wrenching and raw, with a lived power that is strong and soft, passionate and alive, evocative, mystical and exquisite. Your heart will soar and sing, set free from all

*that binds you, and you will find yourself, suddenly, alive
and in love. Haunting and ecstatic, Absolution will live on in
your body, and you will find yourself returning to its depths
again and again. Absolution is a masterful prayer shawl of
passion; wrap yourself warmly in it.*

—Rev. Vivian Gruenenfelder,
Senior Zen Buddhist Monk,
The Order of Buddhist Contemplatives

ABSOLUTION
poetry

Nancy Diamante Bonazzoli

LUMINARE PRESS

www.luminarepress.com

Absolution
Copyright © 2019 Nancy Diamante Bonazzoli

Printed in the United States of America

Cover Design: Melissa K. Thomas

Luminare Press
442 Charnelton St.
Eugene, OR 97401
www.luminarepress.com

LCCN: 2019914756
ISBN: 978-1-64388-233-8

*~ **For all whom I have ever loved** ~*

*May all beings continue to grow
both in wisdom and in Love.*

—Nancy

CONTENTS

DAILY BREAD

LOVE'S BLESSINGS

FORWARD

Of course, I did not know ahead of time the many twists and turns my life would take when I began writing these poems. None of us is that blessed (or cursed!) But I did sense that I must somehow learn to accept and perhaps even welcome what was being given. That instead of destroying me, this unconditional acceptance might very well serve as a means to my spiritual growth.

This coming to 'acceptance of whatever is' has been a long road, sometimes rocky and filled with despair—sometimes overflowing with felt awe and grace. It has often been a painful journey, as such things invariably are, and yet it has also proven spiritually transformative.

I am a weaver and a hand-spinner who loves the sensuous feel of animal fibers slipping through my fingers; the rhythmic flow and full silence of this art touches something deep within me. I feel like a lover, fingering the raw wool while softly inviting the soul of the animal into my very being.

This too is how I write. I start with an image, perhaps only a word or two, a phrase or a memory, and then invite it to come deeply into me, beckoning it to move me. I typically have no idea how or where the words will lead. Only that I feel a pressure begging to be released—a call my pen must answer.

The Divine has been, and is, my Paraclete. I am grateful for everything that my life is and has been. *Everything.*

These poems have been lived. This book is meant to be
of benefit. I hope that you find something helpful within
these pages.

—Nancy

 Nancy Diamante Bonazzoli

HOMEWARD

The view from where I sit
is all that I am
and all that we've sown for ourselves.

Porch chairs rock to the wind's
speaking to itself
and each day
the sun leaves
carrying its glory on its back.

We, the keepers of the legacy
rake crisp leaves into neat stacks
that burn hot
ashes to ashes
dust to dust
my forehead still stained.

It takes whole lives
to get back
to where you started from.

My Father's voice calls
from the night owl's pulpit,
incense curls
while pale curtains tremble
and the golden candle creeps away
without ever looking back.

Some dreams
take it all out of you.
You forget your way—

others give, instead,
like thick jam
on daily bread,
held ever before you
like a blessing.

          Nancy Diamante Bonazzoli

SOME DREAMS . . .

DESPAIR

It moves in
   slowly
            whirling
      like fog
      settling cold misty clamminess
          in deep
                hollows.

My soil is barren.

I can grow nothing
without you
except despair
which attaches itself
like lichens
to the stone caverns of my heart.

I tried to lift
a rosary
to my lips
to call your name
but all that sounded
were the low-wailed
anguished cries
of a child
thought deserted.

I taste your blood in my tears.

          Nancy Diamante Bonazzoli

I marked the page
in the book
where you called *me*
   beloved.
I searched the portrait
   for your smile

but all I can see
is your blood
dripping truth
and clotting
in the muck
before me.

THE BOOK

He locked her in the back shed in Albuquerque in one
hundred degree heat—
left her there a week or more or less
with water of course (they didn't want her dead) but no food

no foolish ideas no willfulness would let her out
her mother would never come, but *he* came with his book
once each day
asking if she had thought about her sins

she would say *no* though she had thought
long into the night when it had cooled and she
could think at all and she would wonder what those words
meant really

words that he spat at her like pigheaded
like penance like willfulness and she would
question things like why

they didn't want her stubbornness
her extra fat
around the middle

they didn't want her
he was a pillar of the church
though her can overflowed she must realize what her

   Nancy Diamante Bonazzoli

sins were or she wouldn't come out
yet the bugs did and the rats did at dusk
especially when the night was darkest

the other day she turned sixty five
and the shade moved while she waited
in my car in the heat with the doors locked

the windows up and when I came back
from getting the milk I found her
crying for the keys

she clenched in her hand and
the book, the book
the book.

PRECIPICE

In truth
there is none
but Silence
which comprehends us
though we
like spotted starlings'
so many voices
like to claim
we know
it
  all.

Such is life
  delusion.

And yet, at times
a creeping doubt
embraces,
a painful gnaw
a crushing ache
through loin
and mind and heart

chastens what we've been
enough
to humble what we've known
until
we're less afraid to look
and more inclined to listen,
held womb-like by

       Nancy Diamante Bonazzoli

such wet despair.
I stand on the precipice,
hands numb, face dripping
turned
into the howling wind

I want to feel.

Will it take
a desperate hurl
of all I've been
a sloughing off
of liberties
for freedom?

Like Sampson will I
use my strength
to yank the chains
that bind me to
my temple's pillars

to crush upon me
this and that
and die intact
alive within
the vision?

Or is there another way?

DANCING BACKWARDS

In that first worn photograph I saw myself
dancing backwards
from the place
I later died. You
were there too, singing,
and in the next your arms
around my waist around
my heart. I never would have guessed
we would suffocate
together
in that place
just one year later.

As you lay dying I remembered light,
just couldn't find it again. Of course,
I hadn't realized then
I too was dying.
That came later.

The canary entered the coal mine
likely against its will.
Day after day. I suppose
many days it made it out alive. But the darkness
and the coal dust and the groans of the men
as they dug
deeper and deeper
into the black void
must have made it afraid.

          Nancy Diamante Bonazzoli

Eventually it gasped.
Breathless.
Fell.
Hard.
We all know the story.
Gassed.

The paramedics
said that you had self-destructed
or something like that. Something about tying your tie
too tight. I guess some big thing inside you simply burst.
I never saw it coming.

They did all that they could of course
but when the shade is pulled down
it's down.
And on the day you burst
I imploded.

       There were only two photographs.

I've lost my shadow. Its not
lost, as if it could be found again
but *lost* lost.
Irretrievable.
Gone.

I wonder sometimes where the good is
that we're told comes from everything. Isn't
that what we're taught, that every cloud has
a silver lining?

There were no silver linings
inside of those coal mines. Only dust
thick
        black
                ashen
                        dust
and a cage

and eventually,
because it often comes down to this,
a singing bird was silenced.

     Nancy Diamante Bonazzoli

THE EVENING THAT LOVE REBIRTHED LOVE

On the eve of the Monday that Mr. Z died
we sat perched on my back deck
your hand enclosing mine as we looked up
at the stars.
You pointed at one star,
then another, urging,

"Up there,"
There is Mr. Z."

My eyes kept flooding, obscuring my vision. Still,
you pointed them out, softly, gently.

It was all we could do then
look up
try to make out stars
star relationships
name them
make them come alive.

It was the 4th of May.
He had been dead 8 hours.

That spring's evening sky seemed full
of absence.
I could not remember
what you were telling me, could not
hold brightness in my memory. Nothing
was where it belonged.
Later,
leaning against your truck as you readied to go,
I suddenly reached inside the lowered window,
looped my hand through your seat belt strap, and held on
desperately.

"I can't remember the stars," I sobbed.

"You will," you whispered.

"Just give it time."

 Nancy Diamante Bonazzoli

THE FINAL INJECTION

While you lay dying
your head in my lap
caught my tears.

I knew then
how later
I'd be out of my mind.

When your chest stilled
my heart's backdoor slammed shut.
No air escaped from either of us

no sigh.
The shock of you gone quiet
batters my days.

I can barely stand
looking at your house.
I can barely stand.

To me
you were always
a hillside covered in Spring.

ACHE

You have died, and now
my entire yearning
with its enormity
clings
like a stone to a mountain
steadfast, shadowless
with all who surround it
in heartbreak and in bleak despair.

I wonder where all of the deaths
that we don't comprehend live?

When I sit and dwell
in the space that once held you
soft and warm, I know
from whence I was born
though not to what you have returned.

What is it that lies
between yesterday and today?

Oh mercy!
You can only answer me now
through the crackling of the leaves.
Gone is the light by which my heart was read.
And in its place?

      Nancy Diamante Bonazzoli

. . . AND THE EARTH HEAVED

I used to think
you understood Truth—
was convinced,
the abbot said.
So tell me why thoughts
of chalk scraping board
make you wince?

My nerves are shot.
I have lived too much
repulse.

Have you forgotten
how to remember?

We had this
record cold
blast through our town
the other day
killing most of the green
snapping off crowns,
so it seems
there's more than a chance
that all things
will never fully heal.

Today the dead
and the still green dying
were carted away
stacked so full
in the tall brown bin
that I had to heave
my weight upon it
so that I could fit
more
   more
as things were still
all shedding
all sobbing wildly
even the pines.

On TV the other night I saw
a long rectangular truck in Haiti
filled over the brim
with grim colorless limbs
bent and re-bent
folded over themselves
until they were flapping
flag-like
with each bump
each jolting pothole
and my right hand jerked
and I saluted that death car
like John-John.

     Nancy Diamante Bonazzoli

Later on I saw
a few of the dead ones
jump, spill out
as the truck raced a corner;
though because I watched the broadcast
and wasn't fully there
there was no sound around
just silence landing.

But as I've told you,
my mind isn't
as it used to be,
so maybe I dreamed it—
especially the part about
the jumping.

And Truth?
Yes
Truth
Truth
and nothing but—
I thought we knew it,
you and I
though now it seems
that you may think
that Truth
and love
change
based on circumstance.

Do you think that once
one has deeply felt
all that's been lost,
one could still
find the will
to sift through rubble again?

Could one actually find
the glinty thing
in such deep muck
and could it be
just waiting for someone

to pick it up, smile
thumb-flick it high
into the brilliance of the sun
and for a moment become
blinded, become
one for one moment
and forget all
that there is to remember?

Do you think
that Truth has changed
to fit the circumstances?

Do you think
I have?

I'm not just talking about *me*

          Nancy Diamante Bonazzoli

here, you know?
I'm talking about
the way they felt,
all falling over each other

thudding and slapping
and smacking and
how I didn't hear a thing
except later
as my mind was dreaming.

They didn't say, of course
(though I feel it safe to presume)
that all of those hearts were then dumped
into some dark forbidding hole
some tomb
somewhere away
so the stench of their breaking
wouldn't bother anyone
wouldn't remind us
that what had been
is now no more
except for the brokenness
of course
and the lingering stench
and the howls of the villagers
still moving in their tents
still wailing of the loss
and lost
and mangled.

Later on I watched the preacher,
the supposed holier one the one
who seemed so sure that only he knows
how the land lies
watched as he roused rapture
amidst the ruins
raising spirits
by raising hands
and reaching toward the heavens.

Did you see Truth?

No.
I felt it,
as I've felt it before
but his heaven was too high for me to reach.

Do *you* see Truth, priest?

As for me
I'll go back to those awe-filled holes,
to all of those hearts
burst open;
that's where I know it is.

That's where I'll keep digging.

     Nancy Diamante Bonazzoli

FELLED

It didn't happen
the way she had warned—my eyes, poked out
with an umbrella.

It was the storm that did it.

Your silence, your words
stole the warmth
from my ears
while somewhere

a tree fell in the forest.

While we can't seem to talk anymore
or we can't seem to hear,
all of a lifetime and more
grows cold

and though you claim that nothing is different,
that the calm will come
after the storm,
tucked in with the misty darkness,
I smell fear.

CLOISTERED

The sun didn't rise today
though I did.

These days that we feel we've been beaten
prayers do not come—
hearts rendered mute by longing.

Outside
wood smoke rises
slowly
like a tired woman
in a white shroud
who'd prefer to stay dreaming.

Truth is fenced in by question today—
saffron robes
dance in the breeze before me.

Did you notice
last time you touched me?

I am getting old.

     Nancy Diamante Bonazzoli

LOST

What she taught me was
that if you prayed a certain way to a certain saint
whatever had gone missing
would be found

but I know now that it never will be
no matter how many times
I recite that prayer
any prayer
because what's vanished
is buried
deep in flesh stuffed

amidst the millions
and millions
of cells that are
themselves dividing
in order to live

with the bad bugs that are in there too
though it's a mystery to me
as I am
no physician
how they can all thrive
in there and I can still walk around

out here as if nothing at all is the matter
as if I have tumbled through
the bleach wash and come out
sparkling and all I have to do now

is hang myself
on the line to dry
so that I can fold myself
into myself
again and again

back into the cool silence
of the dark drawer
and with one *click*

it'll be done.

     Nancy Diamante Bonazzoli

COLLAPSE

The other night I heard her say,
I'm giving away a kneeler
free.
I don't kneel anymore
when I pray; I mean
does anyone?
It isn't easy…

I felt myself still as my breath seized.
I saw myself fall
collapse
beside my bed
surrendered
elbows perched
palms clasped faith's
tall fingers touching

    Please…..

heart bleeding out
its terrible grief
so often
so completely.

I guess that makes me strange.

I can be a bumbling fool at times
so I said nothing.
But inside
in private
    loneliness
        weeping.

          Nancy Diamante Bonazzoli

PIVOT POINT

You just know when you have had
one of those experiences that
within a fleeting instant
instantly and irrevocably
has changed your life
forever.

Out of the blue
or seemingly
you catch a glimpse
then gasp
and watch
as it processes
elbows linked with the father's
to the waiting arms
of your altar

and before you know it
before you even understand
you've lifted the veil
and married grief
for better or worse
forever.

It is these things
        upon which a heart pivots.

Today while walking
I watched sand
turn into dust and fly.
After a time it was gone.

If even a mountain
does not last
crushed down
with each step
of your sole,
how did I ever believe
that this would?

     Nancy Diamante Bonazzoli

AFTER EFFECTS

Whatever do you now
expect me to do
given I've taken in
such a deep taste of
you

go home
go back
as a matter of fact
breakfast's dry toast
old clock's forward boast
even my beloved dog's antics
with ball all engrossed

now find me in ruins
so hard to feel full
because though lovely still
they're all absent
you.

SURRENDER

I have learned
that I can tolerate
my own terror
and thus I know
that I want only
to be with you again.

Let me fling before you
the jewels of the world
as I strip bare
prostrate myself
unafraid
beneath your flaming sword.

Riddle me with gashes—
plunge deeply
into my heart—

 in your name alone
 I surrender—

through the open wounds
the festering,
grant me the strength
to sever my gangrenous will
and the grace
to allow it to decompose
within the moist womb of your
Love.

        Nancy Diamante Bonazzoli

WITH EACH STEP ...

Lately I've been noticing
how it is
that there are always
at least two possible ways
to scale
a single mountain.

Whether or not we try
depends upon how prepared we are
to leave behind what we think we know
for what we think we do not.

The mountain presents to us
her majesty.

How shall we return as much
to the mountain?

ONCE I WAS AN OYSTER

1.

Disrobed kicked out monk.
He left me terrified;
a bad dream

keeps scaring
every time you think about it
he was not who I thought

he was he was not
who he wanted to be
so nothing was real.

Once I was an oyster[1]
iridescent nacre[2]
resilient, strong

what life lived
in me afterwards
covered the parasite.

Nightmarish.

2.

I've read that water oozes
into even the best made vaults.

     Nancy Diamante Bonazzoli

My father was proud

he purchased one then went one more step
had the shimmering blue casket lid sealed.
You can never be sure.

He'll be fine in there, he said,
which seemed to me to be
without purpose.

I hung my head.
Death never leaves
its casket.

3.

Disgraced monk hurls
worded bombs
destroys twelve years

just like that
tears fall
helpless as rain

float away
forever promises
he never meant to keep.

4.

I am going to beat this, he said
and when I do I am really
 going to do something

with my life.
I nodded
remembered

years ago talks of not
wanting to do, be
anything

we're cursed
with the family curse
don't you know

depression
will kill us all
why bother.

That spring
cancer strutted in
unashamed
over-filled its can
with his time.

     Nancy Diamante Bonazzoli

5.

Innocent soft unsegmented body
not left in some dream I'd had
awakened but

coughed up
I am going to beat this
the wise

travel beyond sorrow
kicking off dust
wearing new tomorrows

perfect pearls.

"In nature, **pearl oysters** (bold text mine) produce natural pearls by covering a minute invading parasite with nacre, not by ingesting a grain of sand.[4] Over the years, the irritating object is covered with enough layers of nacre to form what is known as a pearl. Oyster." (2011, February 18). In *Wikipedia, The Free Encyclopedia*. Retrieved 00:46, March 2, 2011, fromhttp://en.wikipedia.org/w/index.php?title=Oyster&oldid=414557197

"**Nacre** pronounced /ˈneɪkər/[1] or "NAY-kər", also known as **mother of pearl**, is an organic-inorganic <u>composite material</u> produced by some <u>molluscs</u> as an inner <u>shell</u> layer; it is also what makes up <u>pearls</u>. It is very strong, resilient, and <u>iridescent</u>."

Nacre. (2011, February 27). In *Wikipedia, The Free Encyclopedia*. Retrieved 00:45, March 2, 2011, fromhttp://en.wikipedia.org/w/index.php?title=Nacre&oldid=416185620

TATTOO

I write on scraps
magazine cards, junk mail
my own shoulder
left, inked
black image, lettered name

to see that requires
a side view, nudity
you won't see the truth looking
head-on, first glance
it takes guts
to strip the dead
of what shouldn't be forgotten

pen dipped pain dipped
ink blood mixed
twelve years ago was
four years before
ink faded and I
began writing
on scraps of everything
since then instead of *until*
and I began counting
in reverse.

        Nancy Diamante Bonazzoli

THE MAGPIE OF DIVINITY

It was the way she walked
not desolate, forlorn
but as if
          detached
she could penetrate the world
outside of things

mysterious
to some extent
possessed
she held a particular kind of authority
her gaze
to be avoided

alone
always
alone
and yet
authentic in her impeccability
not shunned but still
rejected she held
all the cards

it was in her face
her eyes
that even when daylight dissipated
there ever-burned a radiance
so pristine
so primal
no priest
no Holy Order
could deny the flame

isn't that really how it is
that to hear
we need to quiet
to see we need to notice
to speak we need to silence
and to touch we need to
stir the soul

toss the towering tousled mind
the penchant for unbridled greed
delusion
with its immortal seed
of loneliness
          absolute
and pantomime
the Magpie of Divinity.

     Nancy Diamante Bonazzoli

WRITE YOUR FULL NAME AT THE TOP OF THE PAGE

I know what that priest will say
when I speak these poems
he will say
after a period of time that makes me afraid
after a period of time that causes his eyes
to lower and his lip to curl
he will say *So….*
keep writing
and that is all
he will say
and so
I will be left
to confront myself like a bereft
figure at the back of the hall at noon
and I will have to realize too
how I wanted so much more
from him and I will be left to wonder
I will be left to remember
this way of dismissal
even though it's what I'm used to
after all.

When they used to say *Class Dismissed*
it used to strike me
as kind of funny
kind of odd
as if I ever really had been free

to leave those nuns oh I was
a marked child all throughout
the grades and especially the time
in 4th that I turned
my test paper in too quickly
as she was staring at me
after loudly announcing *Pencils Down!*
so all I then
could scribble
were two letters
at the top though I knew
I would be
in trouble somehow
I just knew.

A few days later she stood way up there
passing back those same papers
now graded
we were to keep our hands folded
as in prayer while
our worth was placed
face down
on our desks

   mine never was

so I knew
again I knew
that awful feeling
that woozy ache in my stomach

          Nancy Diamante Bonazzoli

that got so strong
so quickly it started to climb out of my throat
as mine was the only empty desk and my hands
were still folded
as in prayer
as she stood again
unreachable as a god
at the front of the room
holding that last paper up my paper
and she announced loudly as if the Lord herself
were thundering

N.B.—NOBODY

I heard it then
I felt
the ripping sounds and watched
the pieces fall I saw them
snowing up the floor and didn't dare
take my leaking eyes off them as
the twenty three laughing desks kept their white pages
their worth face down their hands
now curled into fists I didn't dare
blink or watch them
it would have driven me mad.

So what do you mean,
Keep writing?

Is that *all* that you can say?

LAMENTATION

I am so confused.

I don't know why
I should believe you love me
when I wake and find
you've trampled
my spring tulips
with your storms
and left them
necks broken
faces smashed
covered in muck.

We had planted them together.

I don't know how
I can believe you
when you tell me
there is no separation,
that you and I are one
always were
always will be
and yet

you've never even had me
to your house
except in a dream.

          Nancy Diamante Bonazzoli

And why must you always keep
so many women?

I've heard you say
a dozen times
you love them all
and no,
you won't leave any of them
ever
and yet

does that really leave time
and love enough
for me?

Why must I always kiss you
secretly
in the woods
in my soft bed?
Why can't I kiss you blatantly
passionately
in front of everyone
wax and wane ecstatically of our love
to all the neighbors?

They know nothing
of what I feel.
They'd think I'm crazy.

This dark night
I sit here chilled;
the warmth of your touch
would be so welcome.
I wish that you
would come,
throw a log upon the fire
and sit with me,
if only for a bit
to kindle my flame.

Do you prefer it this way,
this ever-burning
silent passion?

Then let me
immolate
myself
before you
make ash
of the arrogance
of my weeping.

    Nancy Diamante Bonazzoli

Maybe then
when I am breathed by you
I will finally
certainly
know you for who you are
and thereby know
myself.

TORN

Where will I find
the means to endure?

Under what stump
what stone
might that jeweled fortitude lie?

Within what heart
what new life
might I find reason
for the way I might live?

Can my desolate heart
still pulse
for two?

Will it ever
again tremble?

     Nancy Diamante Bonazzoli

WET PANES

Listen

Rain

drumming angry fingers
on cold transparent panes
that cracked
one Sunday long ago
as he hammered
too close
too hard
for its constitution.

No wonder it all shattered.

Since then
they've worn a half-moon frown
and now

I'm just too tired

to sweep yesterday's ash
and start anew
stack twigs just so
strip news
until my hands are black with ink
and longing
all for a fire.

So be it.

I'll just sit here cold
watch darkness fall like a damned man's halo
and let the silence tell it
though I still hear the wind sighing
and it makes me wonder

Why do the branches continue to beat
already beaten clapboards?

SELF-QUESTIONING

So, this life that you've chosen—
this getting up in the morning
going to work
feeding the kids
staying married

what a heck of a lot of work

trying to forget about pain
trying to remember life before it
not admitting your depression.

How do you answer yourself
those sleepless nights
tossing
turning,
wondering?

Did you cash your hand in early
seeking wealth, comfort
safety or glory?

Did you aimlessly wander?
Do you restlessly regret?

Has your true nature been expressed?
Have you shared with others?
Have you been a humble, gentle
lover of the world?
Have you cultivated wisdom? Goodness?
        Have you even tried?

So, this life that you've chosen—
how *have* you lived it?
How *will* you live it
   until you leave it?

REFUGE

for Andrew

Does it really help
when I steal deftly
into your shade-darkened room
and clasp your warm limp hand
steadfastly
while you are off
exploring distant lands?

Does it really help
all that training
in ministry, psychology
when I sit
with no words
but send my wavering smile off
to float behind
the fevered glaze
of your eyes?

Sometimes we pray
at least I do
not for things, mind you,
or even for
a change in plans
a new itinerary
but for courage
humility
acceptance
patience.

Sometimes I feel
so vulnerable
ego wanting some proof
some reward
or confirmation
that any of this matters.

You shift slightly.
I place a pillow under the small
curve of your hip
(a bit of burden eased
or so it seems.)

My hand sweeps
tempting the loneliness from your cheek.

I shift, slightly
uncross my legs and begin to breathe
with you
quietly
reverently
facing dawn.

    Nancy Diamante Bonazzoli

OH, MY DEAR BROTHER

for Brian

Will I see you again I whispered
half thank you
half amen
while bright ochre leaves waved
against cerulean sky and Fall breezes
fluttered the hope
that licked my face
like a stray dog's
eyes.

I can't know for sure
but I feel you again
in the comings of winter.
I hold you wool sweater wrapped
around what death
has left.
I try not to replace
your laughter
with ache.

I thought that rapid acceleration meant

                          soaring
                  flying
           hurtling
joy

not me
left with the dust
weeping
this ashen dust
all I have left of you.

Where are you?!

Oh, my dear brother,
will we meet again?
Will you come to me again?
Can you show me something
anything
of yesterday's tomorrows?

DAILY BREAD

LYING WITH THE BELOVED

There is no need
to knock, my love.
I have left the door open.

A small blue candle
stands on the oiled bench,
its flame erect
and waiting
to dance your shadow
throughout
my living
room.

I have perfumed the air
with incense,
and whispered the sweet nothings
whose passion once carved
curled letters
in the polished banister
rooted at the stairway
of my becoming.

I lie here naked,
hungry for the sound
of your footsteps
in my hall
my flushed skin
shimmering
with the heat.

64   *Nancy Diamante Bonazzoli*

The mind
can be
a fickle thing.
How precious my remembrance
of you
inside me.
How often I forget.

CONSOLATION

When you try to scream
half in
half out
of sleep
and paralyzed
realize
you've lost your voice

just before you make
yourself wake

   wait

you'll find me there.

    Nancy Diamante Bonazzoli

BECOMING

You stand before me
knee deep
in the karma
of illness

you may not soon
be over it;
it may take eons
to recover completely

but along the way
if you're careful you will slip
steadfastly out of yourself
and into the arms
of your long-lost lover

you ask me,
How can you know this?
for life's fever
has veiled
your seeing
created clouds
of ashen dust
that suffocate your soul

I answer
that you must merely sit
and *be*
  the illness

let it sink you
without struggling
far into your
 own
   murky
     depths

sense the heaviness
the stench
accept its current

for in the muck
of tangled weeds
you will find
that though teardrops
feel like oceans
to those drowning,
they cause the eyes
to sparkle

we can't always
choose
our times
of silence
nor force
a wait
upon the tears

but we *can* decide
how we will cry
and when
it's time
to trade it all

for bowing.

SYNTHESIS

As the moon rose
we spoke
of joy
and of a tired sadness

    spring flowers

       falling snow

 Nancy Diamante Bonazzoli

FORGIVENESS

It has been so long
so long after that day's
bitter tears so long
now I have forgotten
your face

listen

all of those things I said
how old must we be
to reach where memories
live on wildly free
blessedly erased of everything

but their sweetest juicy plums.

TELL ME HOW YOU PRAY

If you sit quietly
in front of your wooden wall
death will come

and the sweet spring dew
will be yours
with the golden nectar
and you will know yourself as deity
and your life
a sacred viaticum.

Tell me how you pray

whether the rosary craves your fingers;
does the still gong
long for its sound?
Does the smoky incense pine
to carry your words to the heavens?
Do you kiss your way each morning
into such a forest of love?

Tell me how you pray

Have you come to terms with life?
Have you dreamed this night?
It is like no other.
It is nothing special.

     Nancy Diamante Bonazzoli

I know, too
that we're all lovers of a sort,
though our embrace
is praying
and our bed
this place,
and it is our single breath
which so sustains us.

FOREST MURMURS

The hallowed woods
envelop me.
Birds call out
while the silent centipede
completes walking meditation
on a carpet of
  crushed
    brown
      leaves.

Kneeling before a pine,
forehead against dark bark
I am jolted by
the majesty of Truth.

Sunlight bullies its way in
unafraid
but the cool reigning darkness
is my most beloved.

How I love this carnal glory.
Life and death and life again
unfurling,
smells of decay and blooming lilies
shy young ferns huddled together
as elder pines recall their stories

     Nancy Diamante Bonazzoli

and
    Oh!
that cracking, splitting
canopy of vital foliage,
how it moans!

Such poetry here
in this virgin forest.
Kissing the ground
I press my ear into the earth,
      shivering
         as it whispers.

INSEPARABLE

Quiet descends.

All retreat
to their crafted lairs
as the evening sun sinks
and bleeds, expands,
seeps throughout the endless sky
while all that it penetrates
comes fully alive;
when shadow-less dusk pulls
its curtain aside
the moonless sky revels.

Among countless planets
in that timeless abyss
two stars pulse
with bliss, as one,
and penetrated
with ineffable
wisdom and trust
hold nothing back,
then burn themselves up,
with omniscient, selfless

Love.

     Nancy Diamante Bonazzoli

LEARN AND LIVE

I have heard
that *being* Love
will lead to the cessation of suffering.
Thus I am left wondering

How hard can it be?

If we bowed to each other,
spoke less
thought more
bathed each day in Your teachings before meeting the world

placed our anger at the altar and left
the dust of delusion with our sandals
outside the door

if we cared less about glory
and more about communion

if the hunger of others
caused *us* to ache

if we dared to fully meet
each other's eyes

if we loved ourselves
as we never thought we *could* be loved

if we took the time each day
to know You
feel You
and while aging
cultivated wisdom

what a web of golden threads we would weave
what majesty

human hearts fully open
joyful in recognizing
this
        our *shared* divinity.

SITTING

Every evening
in my own way,
the way
that feels
most sacred,
I sit
        joining my hands

and it flows.

It flows
      flows
           flows

and just like the harvest moon
the firefly
at dusk in June
my heart glows.

Don't kid yourself.
The world is full
of this and that
such numerous distractions
grief and gladness
ebb and flow.

Just let them go.

Let
        go.

Just sit.
        Joining your hands.

          Nancy Diamante Bonazzoli

BORDER CALL

We have been wandering these forests
forever, don't you see,
and they are still beautiful
beyond beautiful
as is our pendulous striding
when we look
beyond judgment.

These trees
these forests
that we walk and love
love us back
just as intensely;

the trees seed
new trees
all of the time
by subsequence
and each seed
sees our awakening
as clearly as its own.

Do you believe this?

We beings flow along
as one
with One
and if we know this
we can more than imagine
the untold numbers
neatly thread-tied
within us
   as it has always been.

At night
I wake
to sounds
that are not there
knocking,
muffled voices
my own heart beating.

Nothing is familiar
yet it is all that I have ever known.

   How is this?

When I walk without shadow
the floor does not creak
and I see you
without seeing.

What I listen to here
is what the moonlight's reflection

     Nancy Diamante Bonazzoli

stirs from the dust
   timeless songs.

What I see here
is what I have always known;
previews of my own death
so many times over
   so many reasons why.

We think that what has passed away
has gone
and that if we can also forget
all the better.

   But it is not like this.

The midnight's bats
just hide
come dawn
upside down in attics
and deserted places.

Come shadowless dusk
try to catch one
and destroy it.

You will fail .

Their frantic wings keep the wheel turning.

ORDINARY AUTUMN WALK

Late autumn sun warms my shoulders
while the day's perfume
decay and damp cedars
intoxicates

and the way the light fades
like a candle
rhapsodizing about extinction
arouses in me
an urge
to fly.

While I twirl giddily
arms outstretched
in alleluia
my boots sink and crunch,
composting
last summer's glory.

The black dog leaps
pirouettes
she too
three sheets to the wind
with it all.

It is within these moments
that I go nowhere fast,
feel myself tossed

     Nancy Diamante Bonazzoli

like a copper penny
into a leaf rioted pond
heads up,
then stilled.

Oh, what a privilege!
How I'd love
to bottle up
this awe filled
ordinary autumn walk,

carry it always
in pilgrimage
as sacred balm

to annoint
drop by drop
the sleepwalkers
who
in carefully cocooned
memory care units
have forgotten
how to fully live.

OLD GROWTH FOREST

I don't want to touch you
only through a priest
in a temple.

Come run with me
into deep virgin forests
our faces damp
and misty
our bodies swaying
passionately
like dense ferns
in breeze-swept underbrush
  so silent,
    reverent.

Come lie with me
again
  again
root your seed
sum and substance
while canopied leaves shelter us
we'll draw sustenance
from the fertile soil
of each other's
depths.

     Nancy Diamante Bonazzoli

My lips
soften with each whisper
of your homage;
my pores
open to the warmth of you

your smell
brings me
to my knees!

Oh my beloved!
How precious
these lives
of lovemaking.

How sad, those who do not yet feel
your love

lone pennies
dropped into the poor box
just outside
nirvana.

EVEN THE DEAD STUMPS DANCED

I sat shrouded
for I don't know how long
in a hollow
in a temple
of cedars

while tender breezes
tickled the dandelions heads
and sun-struck grasshoppers
catapulted
off of supple stems.

After a time
eyes and heart
lifted from myself
and silence
crept under my blanket
to warm me.

All of my fear
and all of my dreams
all of my self

divested of all consciousness

    breathed

       Nancy Diamante Bonazzoli

and was breathed back
into the great forest

and we laughed together
as that was all there was left to do
while the warmth
  oozed
    melded
and even the dead stumps danced.

THE QUEST

Gratitude flows from me
like honey
thick with gold.

Every day I walk
weaving footsteps
here
there
on deep paths carved
by ancient masters.

How could I
have forgotten
you?

You
whose sweet dew
moistens
my leaves

and you
whom I used to call
Windy
as a child

     Nancy Diamante Bonazzoli

until I grew
and let another lover
take me
almost break me.

Oh! My Divine!
Great compassionate flame
within my embers!
All along we have been
one
yet I have been
so long
wandering,
          searching
so far
for you.

No shame.

It is
as it
is.

No thing.
No one.
No blood-stained cloaks
of purity
to keep me warm.

Merely an unwashed corpse
rotting
in the Western sun.

 Nancy Diamante Bonazzoli

STILL BLESSED

Sun rises.

Snow melts.

Hints of warmth
fever our bootstrapped desire
to squeeze
sniff
cool damp earth

to remember
in gratitude

We are alive!

Though the pond has frozen
the goldfish still live.

Spring.

SELF ABANDONMENT

Abandon all hope!

I've lost
my self
in you.

You
are in all
that I am
and *I*

I've loved you
slept with you
wept with you
but

I didn't know you
when I knew you

instead
like a fool I wandered
while my mind
concealed you

though now
my whole being trembles
with the heat
of your touch

          Nancy Diamante Bonazzoli

it is
through breathing
I receive you

it is my
whole being
that is within you

swallowed up
like Jonah
  alive!

living
in the belly
of your smile.

YES

You said
she's with you
always
as you gestured toward your heart.

That's how it is
with some of us
once impaled
by another's love.

 Nancy Diamante Bonazzoli

VULCAN PEAK

There's no getting around it
even squirrels lead with their heads
and trees have heads for two

one looking down
deep
 deep
  deeply
   down
into and through
moist black earth
and the other arched
gazing upward
unmediated.

It is only if the wind talks too much
too loudly
or perhaps when it believes it has seen enough
that the tree may finally tire
lie down
arms outstretched
to look no more.

All things, given time, lose their innocence.

Yesterday I saw a scrub pine
a Whitebark perhaps,
about four feet high and scraggly
clutching to shale on a cliff.
Only its head bore needles.
The rest of it lay scattered
in varying states of undress;
coarsely amputated appendages
bleached white bones
sentineled
on butterscotch boulders
bright in the blue sky morning's light.

Gazing deeply
I reflected
   me
backpack and stomach full
heart and spirit soaring
   and this lone pine
cemented into unmovable ledge
thin as a razor's edge
tenaciously existing.

 Nancy Diamante Bonazzoli

Barely breathing
I paused

and for some ineffable infinitude felt my heart leap
into that pine and my fullness pour
out and through
its hardened center.

Yet today
like the loss of breath that etched
those fallen limbs into memory
I wonder

whose heart really was it that leapt?

MEDITATION

Keep practicing.

I know there will come a time
when mist sweeps past
revealing lovers
fully in union.

All those dawns
evenings
sitting
focusing
  not focusing

a place on the wall
undefined
except by faithfulness.

Restless body
anxious mind
calming
  calming

breathe in
and through
the sweet aroma
the heart
glowing
  moving

　　　　Nancy Diamante Bonazzoli

serpents dancing by moonlight.

            Clouds wisp past.
soft crescent moons
of consciousness
                        thrust
disappear
                    fill
empty

        bliss.

WITHIN THE FOLDS OF NIGHT

As I walk along
all vague and indefinite
so unacceptably without aim
I suddenly see that everything
that was ruined within me
has risen
called forth from shame.

I see that Faith is found
not so much in the light
that burns
but within the folds of night

for even when enveloped
in terrible darkness
our anguished cries
are heard.

I cannot possess life,
though I have surely tried.
Life possesses me

and memories live
where memories live
in quiet gauzy rooms
curtained
by time.

    Nancy Diamante Bonazzoli

Night shadows daylight
though we don't often
hear that said.
We cannot choose
to taste of Mystery

we must be chosen instead
bequeathed a kiss
that lays us open
fully revealed.

I will no longer lament
How am I to live
but will let the living
live me

cease striving with personal aim
accept my cup
drink whatever it contains
allow its elixir to exhilarate.

I will rise from the bench
carry the temple home
waft the perfume of His glory
and name
everywhere
anointing every story

   like Springtime.

     Nancy Diamante Bonazzoli

LOVE'S BLESSINGS

I LONG TO KNOW YOU

Come
give me your hand
let us sit together wrapped
in arms and night and dreams

for dreams
are just dreams
yet such necessary things
for what we cannot imagine
we tend not
to believe

like love

that temptress
who fingers our hearts
with her own silent longing

like prayer

prayer is a circle
as is forever
as is love

     Nancy Diamante Bonazzoli

as is love
prayer's intercourse
for when together
they startle hearts
from their torpor

last night's cool breath wept glad
madness upon browning ferns
while fog
milky thick as cataracts
faintly blew its mossy petrichor
through our cracked window
thrilling my senses

yet though I slept not
I dreamed
of a rose at bloom
in winter, blood
red in its bed
of warm snow

only snow
and blood red rose
and I was filled

by this dream of possible
impossibilities,
a squirrel's cache

in paradise
never looked so rich
nor you

please
come to me some night
take my hand
let us sit together wrapped
in arms and night and dreams
and tell me *your* dreams
don't hold back

sometime tell me
what bounty the sea has fetched
what broken shells tide has kicked
swept
tell me of the sand dollar's
worth
what a tumbling stones' unrest
unearthed

tell me what alone sounds like
what joy tastes like
what fear feels like what grace
looks like what writing
smells like and what you
don't like
and do

     Nancy Diamante Bonazzoli

tell me what prayers kiss
your lips what dreams dream
your dreams
what it is wholly
that salt winds have whipped

just please
don't tell me *oh nothing*
it was just
a nice time
away
  alone

I long to know you.

DON'T BE SO AFRAID

Hurt is a promise
we make to each other.
Each kiss
another vow.

It can't be otherwise

as within the anguish of our inner impoverishment
bereft though we seem
we are seen.

   I still believe in the Promised Land.

In time, in sun
frosting melts
revealing sweetness
plain and good and worthy.

And love does not beget love
without crucifixion.

   So, take my hand—

Must we follow a prescriptive?

Moonlight lives its own glow
whether visible beyond itself
or to itself
or not

as does faith
as does trust
as does benedicite

  as does Love.

WHAT IS THERE TO FEAR?

A caress
is more acceptance
than insistence
more surrender
than command
more prayer
than question

so please

help my fingers kiss
your heart
let them reach
redress
with a potter's finesse
the once neglected clay
of your body.

Rest.

I have prayer enough
to hold you.

Let love become
your habit.

Don't hide
wearing winter's cloak

   Nancy Diamante Bonazzoli

like Fall maples
divested of dress
like Adam and Eve
like secrets.

God shrouds
each soul's fullness
with His own

do you believe this?

with His own
so what is there to fear?

Help
I whisper
Guide me
to the only one who can speak
to the part of me that knows

and taking my fingers in His own
we smooth
pull
infuse
'till all fear
is vanquished
'till you ooze
spread wildly

kaleidoscopically
and with fierce abandon
greet each morning
like sunrise.

     Nancy Diamante Bonazzoli

LOVING A SOLITARY

White sheep slip
under crescent moon
refusing to be counted

Wide-eyed lambs thrust
lips seeking teats
amidst heady lanolin darkness

Restless ewe
by full moon
her milk spent

Christ hallowed the mustard seed
in parables
weed though it be—
unwanted
according to its intent

And you?
I hope you can understand

I need nights
to which I wake
with hymns stolen from a dream
on my lips
and not you

I'm sorry
Do I sound cold?

You might think these
the words of a woman grown
too lean from solitude
for you

But no

Let me tell you

There is a place I can take you
when we join,
a wellspring
never drunk alone

a water
parted,
both sides wet with blessing
always

come closer.

Kiss all that lies within me

     Nancy Diamante Bonazzoli

I tell you
it's just the sign of the cross
of loving a solitary.
What you see as walls

  come closer
   come closer

Look

only a dream.

BIRDSONG IN TREES

When I glance
surreptitiously,
pretending
not to,
I see you there
absorbed,
anointed with
this precious moment's
grace

last night's holding
once we had stilled, oh
how my legs, arms
couldn't let go
as my palms stroked your back,
committing our music
to memory

and oh,
how I haven't let go
still and so
as you work quietly
across the hall
my heart beams
love kisses

     Nancy Diamante Bonazzoli

and you, absorbed,
nonetheless
feel kissed
I know you must
for my heart's silent prayers
shroud, envelop,
echoing their refrain

"Oh gratitude,
        deep gratitude"

and this sacred song
resounds sweetly all around

like birdsong in trees.

THIS MORNING, I WISH I HAD INSISTED UPON TIME TO EXPLAIN.....

Did you miss me last night
lying alone in your bed, you asked

well, I said, *if truth be told,*
no

no thoughts of you
kept me restless
though the pillow where you had lain
caressed my face with your scent
so what was there to miss

today, when pale shades opened
revealing morning light
I confess
I wanted to see *your* eyes shining;
when I smelled coffee
brewing heady with awakening
I wanted to nuzzle *you*
drink *you* in
as elixir for my day

though my day was joyful
though I did not miss you
like poets speak of missing
like craving
like pain
like can't live without

                Nancy Diamante Bonazzoli

but I missed you
not like in loss
not like when lightening picks
from a whole sky
the tallest tree
to rip its passion through
burns itself out
then disappears
but I missed you with surety
with steady quiet rhythm

I missed you
like you know how in dreams there is
no time or space or distance
no engulfment
how in dreams we can be here and there
and everywhere without intent
without ever worrying about how
we've gotten where we are
or whether it's right

it's just a given
it's just faith in the dream
that you don't even realize
is a dream
well, that's how I feel

your touch lingers
your scent holds
when you are not here
and closing my eyes
I see your smile
feel your arms holding
feel your fingers exploring
so I am not lonely
with missing

it's not like that
but ever since you first walked in
all chaste shirt and polished
all furtive glances and carefully wrapped heart
I've missed you

what I hadn't even known I'd missed
I missed
something deep stirred
something forgotten
something sacred
unabashed
that smile before The Apple
perhaps

     Nancy Diamante Bonazzoli

who knows why
long barren soil
suddenly notices sun
then seed
sits up straight
and blooms

that's a question best left
to gods

so yes, I miss you
now go home
and be without me, be
full without me and
time will fly
or not
and we will find
perhaps meaning
perhaps synchronicity
perhaps more

or perhaps less
even though
that's hard to imagine
it could be truth
we can't know that
yet

see, this is what it means to receive
each day
as palette of offering
and this is what it means
to embrace all
as grace
which is, of course
not always easy

yet, this is the thing

even if we never again share
such communion, even if no
communicants remain
for whatever reason
even if you tell me no
or I tell you no
you should know

hell, I just want you to know

that for me there's been no madness about it
no
it's been more of a quiet thing
a humble thing
a growing awe
begging to know itself

     Nancy Diamante Bonazzoli

so imagine this

imagine soft fingers caressing palms,
fingers, tips all
circling moving
up wrist and forearm imagine

fingered tendrils spiraling
twining around and through dark chasms
fingering lace and curls
tugging tassels
lazily parting
lips half open
half revealing
urging
more of a thing
than can be seen
a thing to be savored
a thing for each moment
a bliss

imagine this
I miss you
oh how I miss you
but even if I should die
before I wake
know

the jewel of journeying thus far with you
will forever remain
a bright thing
a sacred thing
that infused my being with gratitude

this is how I see it.

This morning,
I wish I had insisted upon time to explain….

MIA CARA

My desire
is that we will make
of our two lives
one long love poem
that you will delight
in singing with me
all of our nights and days.

My desire
is that each day
together we will wake
sensitively nurture
intimately embrace
each other as blessing
as grace.

My desire is *you*....

You, my desire
will pray with me
whisper to me passionately
hold me ever tenderly,
we will share our lives,
cherish this our blessing,
and always we will smile

even through life's crying
we will smile.
Hard times will not weaken us,
good times will not mislead us.
As is our souls purpose
we will pray
we will stay *"we."*

My desire is *you*….

     Nancy Diamante Bonazzoli

FIREFLIES

It's certainly not
that I didn't want
to stay

it's just that
sometimes a firefly
shines brightest unseen
un-entwined.

But oh
lingering in your doorway
all tender kisses and starlight

you have no idea.

The soft webs of
your hands
your lips
release animal longing
appeased only
through your touch.

So yes
tonight my house is quiet
and I am still
while in my bed
pulse lightening bug dreams
flashes of longing
of you.

It's said that fireflies
are becoming rarer
these days still
one's enough for me
as are you.

     Nancy Diamante Bonazzoli

QUIET MORNING AFTER

A quiet
      quiet
            morning
this morning

sweet
      silent
            white flakes swirl
melt

dust
      my lips melt
melt

touch
      my cells swirl
still
      holding the warmth of you

A quiet
      quiet
            morning
this morning

sweet.

TERMINAL

Live now
live
with whole being bliss
she'd nuzzle my neck
with whispers as if
once rod had flung
its line towards the sea
it could be halted midair
just by wishes

though that is not what she meant
I've known that since

she meant
long wooded walks
earth's warp and weft
candlelight
moonlight
sound and scent

she meant the hours she spent
in my arms
in my eyes
her dog on our bed and she
on her side
laughing blithely hell bent
at her own seriousness.
(Oh why me, so soul kissed?)

          Nancy Diamante Bonazzoli

she meant encircle limbs tightly
in that meant to be way
even when
especially when
all around us
gives way

she meant not running backwards
out of conditioned fear
but jumping into
through with me
in happiness, *dear*
it's best shared
she would grin

she meant
relishing life
while smiling at death,
she would say,
Look! It's we
who hold on
the tightest

I never could tell
if her passionate tears
leaked from mirth or from wounds
heaped too full
for her years

Life is just life and our
tears are just tears, so
live now
live
with whole being bliss!

I now see the answer
though she'd shrug and deflect

when her line finally broke,
Oh, God
how I wept.

WILL THE WORLD EVER BE MADE WHOLE?

Loving has broken me
    open.

Imagine a city
broiling in stench and din
haunted
with poverty and needles
shaming and hate
heartbreak and destruction.

Yet, new flowers,
seeded within rich black loam
in the garden of our grief,
revivify man's aims
like fertile dreams
tucked faintly shimmering
into the edges
of early morning
awakenings.

Will
  the world ever
    be made whole?

Within our atmosphere
fear
like wind
tussles

the elegy of man and opinion
power and self
we and they
Left and Right.

Songs of Mourning.

Still, kissed by the great mercy
that is grace
tiny blossoms
grow,
glow ever the lovelier
for their humble piety.

But who am I

some manifestation of
spark and conditioning,
some trajectory of
choice and constriction
faith and despair
of attention that peers behind
plans ahead
then loses the dream
in the midst of
such vast in-betweens?

Straddling today and memory
my breath rises,
and eventually

     Nancy Diamante Bonazzoli

swirling wildly
with that of all peoples
   falls
as rain
   or snow
      or cutting ice
as is our choice
   falls
perhaps
   as no thing at all.

We are always given back
what we have sighed out
through faith,
through humble obsecration.
There is never any lack
no separation
outside of mind.

Thus I pray
not *to*
but *through*.

Who am I
but one snowflake,
turning back into itself
once melted upon the tongue
of Love.

FINAL WISH

If I could be blessed with just one wish
before I close my eyes for last
it would have to be
without a doubt
one more repast
of loving you

to lay about
all warm and heady
while sunshine's bed is growing ready
and finally not even shadows remain
only dark waves crashing
beyond the shades

I'd raise my head to kiss your neck
with eyes still closed in bliss's languor
spent and dewy, heaven sent
with all quiescent namelessness
we'd breathe again
one holy breath

before I close my eyes for last
I'll thank the Lord oh, once again
I'll thank Him for His gift
of you and plead
for one last feast
of loving you.

          Nancy Diamante Bonazzoli

UNFATHOMABLE LOVE

Again
as I slept
quiescent
dreamless

you came

kissed my eyes open

and inebriating me
with your perfumed breath
whispered

Come—know me

and I

engorged with you
to my limitless depths
cried out
        then disappeared

carried
beyond suffering

fused

with the timeless nameless benediction
of such unfathomable love.

SO PROFOUNDLY BLESSED

As I walk
through wind and rain
these early autumn days

I *listen.*

Darkened treetops sway and clap;
a throaty Deep South choir prays
not for deliverance
but for benediction
while cool, frosty wetness
caresses
my face, my neck
moves deftly
tenderly
underneath my clothes
melds
with the heat in my chest
in my trembling heart.

Thus I know
I have been baptized
by forest
by silence
into Your very marrow
of Truth.

This soothes me.

     Nancy Diamante Bonazzoli

My gratitude
limitless
as is this knowingness

that should I not come to You daily
in my solitude
I might perish
so perilously
so often do I stand perched
upon the edge of life's abyss.

Such gratitude
for the courage You grant me
to hurl myself
into Your passionate embrace

again and
again and
for the trust and
most importantly for Your love.

Wrapped in Your miracles of wind and rain and sun
I hide for a time
deep within the prayers of love.

Love

permeates my essence
sears my mind
brings me to my knees

with joy
with grief
for all of the much lived suffering
of all
including myself.

I pray now that all beings may feel
Your unfathomable goodness
Your ineffable love
such that from suffering may spring forth
faith
joy
wisdom
such that all may know
Your embrace
Your peace
Your love
such that in all may arise
the most profound gratitude.

May I be empty
of myself. Use me
as an instrument of transformation
that *all* may truly know themselves as beloved
by You
in oneness
with Your Truth.

Oh Sacro Silenzio!
I humbly rejoice!
The quiet cabin within my heart overflows
with Your vast love
Your peace
with the hope
the fervent prayer
that my life
is being well lived
despite my multitude struggles and errors
or even perhaps
because of all that.

Yes.

Yes!!

In spite of all my failings I find *this*
to be the most amazing thing

I have
I continue
each day to be
to know

I am

so profoundly blessed.

ACKNOWLEDGEMENTS

Grateful acknowledgement is made to the editors of the following, in which these poems first appeared:

Sacred Voices: Essential Women's Wisdom Through the Ages by Mary Ford-Grabowsky, 2002, HarperOne, page 296; "Laying with the Beloved" (hereafter known as "Lying with the Beloved"

Ars Medica: A Journal of Medicine, the Arts and Humanities, Vol. 5, No 2, Spring 2009: "Becoming" and "Refuge."

About the Author

Nancy Diamante Bonazzoli was ordained a Zen Buddhist Lay Minister in 2004 and later, in 2007, received Lineage Transmission. Her poems honor her Christian roots yet do not focus on any single religious perspective. Rather, her writing appeals to all who have ever questioned life deeply through the means of suffering, introspection, loss, disappointment, questioning… and, of course, love.

Nancy earned an M.A. in Clinical Psychology from the Fielding Institute and a Doctor of Ministry (D.Min.) degree from Mathew Fox's University of Creation Spirituality. Although she has lived with difficult chronic illness for many years, she voluntarily dedicates herself to helping others experience increasing acceptance, understanding, joy and gratitude within their own multi-faceted lives.

Nancy's work has been published in various journals, as well as in the anthology *Sacred Voices: Essential Women's Wisdom through the Ages* by Mary Ford-Grabowsky, and she is a past winner of the William G. Doody Memorial Prize for Poetry.

Nancy lives in Southern Oregon together with her beloved partner and her precious standard poodle Shanti, a certified therapy dog. Occasionally, as her health allows, she and Shanti volunteer with Asante Hospice and visit nursing homes, assisted living centers, and hospitals as well.

Nancy can be reached at mysticforestrefuge@gmail.com.

www.ingramcontent.com/pod-product-compliance
Lightning Source LLC
Chambersburg PA
CBHW031330060726
47590CB00007B/2421